Aforethinking and Aforebeing

Where the future shapes the present

A theory, a manual,
an epochal shift, and a viable path.
For leaders, strategists, and everyday individuals,
this discipline bridges foresight with action, inspiring unique
strategies from the future through a consciousness shift of
knowledge and applied techniques.

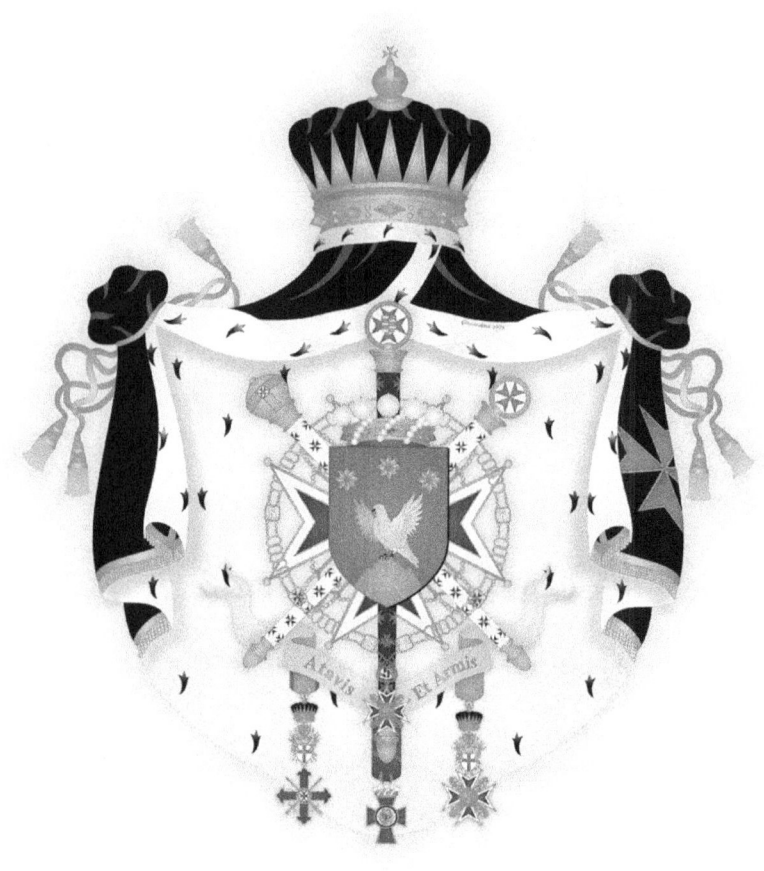

- *Introduction* 7
- *Aforethinking* 9
  - What aforethinking is 9
  - Key Elements of Aforethinking: 9
  - Examples of Aforethinking in Leadership 10
  - Noble Legacy and Aforethinking 13
- *Aforebeing* 15
  - What Aforebeing is 15
- *From Aforethinking to Aforebeing* 18
  - The Art of combining Data and Vision 18
- *A viable path* 20
  - Aforethinking: Strategic Foresight and Planning ... 20
    - Definition: 20
    - Key Focus: 20
  - Steps in Aforethinking: 20
  - Aforebeing: Living in the Future 21
    - Definition: 21
    - Key Focus: 21
  - Steps in Aforebeing: 21
  - Here's how this path unfolds: 22
    - Step 1: Strategic Foresight (Aforethinking) 22
    - Step 2: Visionary Alignment 22
    - Step 3: Behavioural Alignment (Bridging the Gap) 23
    - Step 4: Total Future Immersion (Aforebeing) 24
  - The Benefits of Aforebeing for Strategic Leadership and Planning are multiple. 24
  - Aforethinking is Rooted in Probability 25

Aforebeing is Based on Clear Vision...........................26
The shift: Aforethinking vs. Aforebeing 27
In Practice...27
    Aforethinking in Action:..27
    Aforebeing in Action: 28
    Shifting from Aforethinking to Aforebeing.........28
Aforethinking - to - Aforebeing Framework.................30
    From Strategic Foresight to Visionary Leadership: the ten steps...30
    Phase 1: Aforethinking – Strategic Foresight and Planning 30
    Step 1: Horizon Scanning.....................................30
    Step 2: Scenario Development 30
    Step 3: Strategic Risk Management....................31
    Step 4: Present Action Based on Future Preparedness...31
    Phase 2: Transition to Aforebeing – Commitment to Vision 32
    Step 5: Future Vision Selection 32
    Step 6: Deep Internalization of the Vision 32
    Step 7: Create Strategic Alignment....................33
    Phase 3: Aforebeing – Living in the Future and Controlling the Present 33
    Step 8: Total Mental Immersion in the Future ...33
    Step 9: Control the Present Through Future Vision 34
    Step 10: Leading from the Future 34
Key Distinctions: Aforethinking vs. Aforebeing.............35
Application of the Framework.......................................35
    Aforethinking to Aforebeing Methodology 36
    Define Purpose and Context 36

- Aforethinking: Strategic Foresight and Scenario Building 36
- Transition from Aforethinking to Aforebeing 38
- Aforebeing: Living and Leading from the Future 38
- Leadership and Communication from Aforebeing 39
- Key Outcomes of the Methodology 40

Leading from the Future 42
- Steps from Aforethinking to Aforebeing 43
- Practical Tools for Each Phase 43
- Transition – Committing to a Singular Future 44
- Aforebeing – Living and Leading from the Future 45
- Monitor and Align – Continuous Adjustment 46
- Differentiating Tools for Aforethinking and Aforebeing 46
  - Aforethinking Tools (Probabilities and Flexibility): 46
  - Aforebeing Tools (Certainty and Control): 47

Tools for Aforebeings 48
- Reverse SWOT: Addressing Threats to Secure the Chosen Future 48
- Gantt and Reverse Gantt: A Powerful Tool of Check and Balance 49
  - Alignment as a Strategic Imperative 49
  - Diagnosing and Correcting Misalignment 50
- Strategy example 50
  - Gantt and Reverse Gantt as Continuous Checks 51
  - Practical Example: A Renewable Energy Company's Reverse Gantt 53
- Phases of Reverse Training 66
  - Phase 1: Competency Observation from the Future 66

Phase 2: Defining the Competency Gaps........................67
Phase 3: Action Planning for Skill Development..............68
Phase 4: Managing Workforce Continuity and Turnover 69
Phase 5: Selection and Recruitment for the Future Workforce..69
Point of View: 2030..70
Step 1: Assessing Competencies in 2030.........................71
Step 2: Defining Hard and Soft Skills for 2030 71
Step 3: Planning the Actions for Skills Development (2025-2029) 72
Step 4: Addressing Turnover and Workforce Continuity (2025-2029)..73
Step 5: Selection Parameters for Future HR (2024)..........74

The future is 76

  Bibliography..78

Introduction

It was the holy middle of the winter of 1995, and the Russian cold was bone-chilling—the kind of cold that makes you appreciate a good coat and a sip of vodka. But while the temperature outside was freezing, the heat around the speculations on the rouble was intense. The Russian economy was in a tailspin, caught in an inflationary spiral, and the rouble seemed to be losing value by the second.

In the midst of this economic storm, I found myself working with the Minister of Finance to find a way out of the crisis. We needed more than a quick fix; we needed a monetary solution that would break the inflationary spiral and restore confidence. Together, we devised a plan to reduce the monetary mass of roubles in circulation by converting part of the wealth into more stable currencies like the dollar, pound, and German mark.

Our strategy involved revamping a joint venture between INA (Istituto Nazionale Assicurazioni), Italy's state insurance company, and Rosgosstrakh, the Russian State Insurance Company, which managed the retirement funds of Russia's state workers. This joint venture was re-envisioned as an investment firm, directing the social security deductions from Russian state workers into a fund based in London. By investing in dollar- and pound-denominated markets, we stabilized part of Russia's wealth, effectively breaking the inflationary cycle of the rouble.

As we worked through the crisis, I relied on aforethinking — analysing market trends, historical patterns, and fiscal realities to craft a strategy that aligned with the most probable outcomes. It wasn't just about responding to the crisis but planning for the future we could foresee, based on solid data and strategic foresight.

But something else emerged as we moved forward: a growing sense of *aforebeing*.

It wasn't just about imagining that future; it felt as though we were already fully present in it—not just mentally, but with all our senses, reason, and emotions. We could see the stabilized economy, feel the confidence returning, and act as though we were living in that future state. We weren't just preparing for the future; we were inhabiting it already, acting as if the present was the past of that future. It's a mindset that, perhaps, comes naturally to me.
You see, it happens that I am the offspring of a small noble family—one of those long-standing lineages where thinking beyond the present moment is a habit. But not the kind of nobles who've only ever thrived. Nothing like the charming prince. In fact, my ancestors have once literally hanged out of the city walls during a just revolt.

As I like to remember, my family - and personal - history is a blend of grandeur and well-earned humility.

I guess that's where I learned the importance of planning for the long term—even if it's just to avoid another set of angry townspeople!

Joking aside, this background shaped my way of seeing things. Aforebeing—the ability to not only see but truly inhabit the future—feels like something passed down. It isn't just about foresight, it's about engaging the future with all your senses, acting with confidence and certainty because you're already living in the outcome you've envisioned.

This experience showed me how powerful it is to combine aforethinking —strategic foresight grounded in probability — with aforebeing — acting from a future that you already live in.

It wasn't just about managing the present crisis; it was about guiding today's actions from tomorrow. And it worked.

Aforethinking

What aforethinking is

Aforethinking is the discipline of strategically using information to identify and define the most probable future outcome based on available data and trends. It involves gathering and analysing the broadest amount of current and historical data to predict the future that is most likely to unfold, and then aligning our actions to reach that outcome.

Aforethinking is based on calculus and determined decision-making, preparing for the future through a blend of data-driven insight and strategic planning.

The goal is to anticipate and navigate complex scenarios with confidence, using foresight to guide actions that ensure resilience and adaptability.

Key Elements of Aforethinking:

1. Data-Driven Foresight: Grounded in analysis, aforethinking uses trends, projections, and current knowledge to forecast the most likely future scenario.

2. Probability-Based Strategy: The strategist embraces the most probable outcome and structures present actions to align with that future, minimizing risk.

3. Strategic Flexibility: While focused on a probable future, aforethinking incorporates flexibility, allowing for adjustments as new information or unforeseen changes arise.

4. Control through Anticipation: By aligning with the most probable future, aforethinking enables the strategist to

influence the present with foresight, shaping actions to thrive in the anticipated future.

In essence, aforethinking is the art of using today's knowledge to forecast tomorrow's most likely reality, preparing for it through informed, proactive decision-making.

Examples of Aforethinking in Leadership

1. Winston Churchill – Strategic Foresight in War and Politics
- Winston Churchill demonstrated aforethinking during World War II, particularly with his early warnings about the dangers of Nazi Germany long before most European leaders recognized the threat. He did not foresee every detail of the war, but he used his deep understanding of geopolitical patterns and military history to anticipate the most probable outcomes of appeasement.
Churchill's speeches, including his famous "Iron Curtain" speech, reflect his probability-based foresight. He wasn't merely reacting to the 1930s situation but calculating the most likely future conflicts and shaping present actions accordingly. His strong sense of Britain's role as a global power allowed him to act with the confidence of a leader preparing for future realities that were based on a deep understanding of history and emerging trends.

2. Otto von Bismarck – Long-Term Political Strategy
- Otto von Bismarck, the "Iron Chancellor" of Germany, practiced aforethinking through his long-term political strategy. He foresaw the probable future of a unified Germany under Prussian leadership and orchestrated alliances, wars, and diplomatic manoeuvres to align with this vision.
Bismarck's decisions were not speculative; they were based on the most probable outcome of unification over decades. He foresaw not only Germany's unification but also the potential future conflicts that this would bring to Europe. His ability to

construct a diplomatic system to prevent these future wars exemplifies his use of aforethinking, preparing for the most likely political realities and strategically navigating present circumstances to avoid unnecessary conflicts.

3. *John F. Kennedy – The Space Race and Future Vision*
- John F. Kennedy's commitment to space exploration through the Apollo program is an excellent example of aforethinking in leadership. His speech in 1961, promising to land a man on the moon by the end of the decade, was not merely an optimistic vision; it was based on an understanding of the most probable advancements in technology and international competition during the Cold War.
Kennedy acted from a perspective where space exploration was not optional but an inevitable extension of the technological race with the Soviet Union. His ability to secure funding and political support for NASA reflected his strategic foresight - he understood that space dominance would shape global power dynamics, and he aligned present actions with that probable future.

4. *Prince Metternich – Post-Napoleonic Europe and Balance of Power*
- Klemens von Metternich, Austria's foreign minister during the Congress of Vienna in 1815, is a key example of aforethinking. He anticipated the probable future of a post-Napoleonic Europe and recognized that long-term peace depended on maintaining a balance of power across the continent.
Metternich's diplomatic actions—building alliances and establishing borders—were designed to prevent future conflicts, reflecting his understanding of Europe's geopolitical dynamics. His decisions were not just reactive but aligned with a probable future of European stability that he was actively shaping through present treaties and agreements.

5. Mahatma Gandhi – Strategic Patience and Long-Term Vision
- Mahatma Gandhi's leadership of India's independence movement was rooted in aforethinking. He used strategic foresight to predict that non-violent resistance would be the most effective method to achieve independence in the long term.

Gandhi's patience and long-term vision were based on his belief in the most probable outcome of peaceful independence. He recognized that non-violence would not only liberate India but also position the nation as a moral leader on the global stage. His leadership was guided by probability-based foresight, where he saw that ethical resistance would have the greatest impact on shaping India's future and standing in the world.

For noble families and aristocratic leaders, aforethinking is a natural mindset rooted in their long-term responsibility for dynastic legacies. These leaders operate within a historical continuum, where their actions are not just for immediate benefit but part of a multi-generational strategy.

1. Habsburg Dynasty
- The Habsburgs governed with aforethinking, carefully positioning their family to maintain power through strategic marriages and alliances, rather than relying solely on military conquest. Their decisions were calculated based on long-term probabilities, ensuring that the Habsburg name would continue to dominate European politics for generations. Their family motto "Bella gerant alii, tu felix Austria nube" ("Let others wage war, but you, happy Austria, marry") reflected their use of aforethinking to maintain power over the long term, preparing for future dominance through family alliances rather than military might.

2. Medici Family
- The Medici family exercised aforethinking in their patronage of the arts, culture, and politics. By investing in culture and

education, they ensured that their name would be associated with Renaissance greatness long after their political dominance faded. Lorenzo de' Medici strategically invested in artists like Michelangelo, fostering a cultural legacy that would last for centuries, positioning the family as not just political rulers but cultural architects of a future world.

3. House of Windsor (British Royal Family)
- The House of Windsor demonstrates aforethinking through its careful management of the monarchy's role in the modern world. Queen Elizabeth II's handling of various crises reflected her probability-based strategy—she understood that the monarchy's survival depended on evolving with the times while maintaining its traditions. The careful preparation of heirs like Prince William reflects aforethinking, where decisions are made with the future in mind, ensuring that the monarchy remains relevant for the next 100 years.

Noble Legacy and Aforethinking

Nobility, particularly those tied to multi-generational legacies, naturally embodies aforethinking as part of their leadership style. These leaders operate within a timeless perspective, where their actions today are guided by probable outcomes and a desire to ensure long-term success for future generations.

- Genes and Legacy: Nobles, tied to centuries-old lineages, often think and act from a future-oriented perspective, planning for the success of their descendants based on long-term strategic foresight.

- A-Timed Perspective: Their strategies reflect a deep historical consciousness, where actions are not taken for immediate gain but to ensure the continuation of family legacies and estates over centuries.

Aforethinking is a key characteristic of great leaders who embrace probability and make decisions based on the most likely future outcomes. This mindset, prevalent in noble leadership, allows leaders to guide present actions with the knowledge that they are preparing for the most probable future. Leaders like Winston Churchill, the Habsburgs, and Bismarck exemplify this timeless strategic perspective, where present actions are calculated to align with future realities.

This probability-based approach to leadership ensures resilience and adaptability, making aforethinking an essential discipline for noble families and modern leaders alike.

Aforebeing
I saw the angel in the marble and carved until I set him free.

What Aforebeing is

Giorgio Vasari, in his *"The Lives of the Most Excellent Painters, Sculptors, and Architects"* tells us that Michelangelo used to describe his artistic process as "freeing the figure from the stone," implying that the statue already existed within the marble and his role was simply to remove the excess.

This intuition is a glance of aforebeing: the future is not something speculative or unknown, but already realized in the mind of the leader or strategist.

In aforebeing, the present becomes the medium through which the pre-existing future is brought into reality, akin to Michelangelo's chisel uncovering the statue.

Figures such as Einstein and Michelangelo share a characteristic capacity for envisioning the correct solution or future state with intuitive certainty.

Michelangelo's ability to see the statue within the marble is paralleled by Einstein's formulation of relativity, which he described as a sudden insight into a future theory that simply required formalization.

Both figures exhibit aforebeing by mentally inhabiting the realized future before looking at the present from a rear mirror. This is the opposite of the more conventional approach of gradually discovering or testing solutions through trial and error.

Aforebeing implies that the future is not a distant or unknown territory but a concrete reality that exists within the strategist's mental framework. The actions taken in the present are therefore not speculative but inevitable steps toward realizing this future. In this model, certainty replaces fear, as the leader or genius is acting with the knowledge of an outcome already pre-determined.

By embracing aforebeing, the present becomes a process of liberating or revealing the future. Just as Michelangelo removed the excess marble to reveal the statue, this process eliminates present uncertainties to reveal and realize the inevitable future.

Aforebeing is primarily a mindset rather than a formal discipline.

It reflects a particular way of experiencing and perceiving the future—living in it fully with all senses and then acting in the present based on that future certainty. However, from this mindset, a discipline of planning naturally emerges. This discipline is distinct in that it operates with the clarity of hindsight while being rooted in foresight, akin to planning by looking in the rearview mirror. The future is so fully realized in the leader's mind that each action in the present is guided by a perspective of certainty, almost as if the future is the past and all that remains is for the present to catch up.

Aforebeing is fundamentally a state of consciousness which generates action.

This sense of certainty differentiates aforebeing from mere strategic foresight. Whereas aforethinking focuses on probable outcomes derived from trends and data, aforebeing transcends probability by creating an emotional and intellectual alignment with the future.

This mindset allows leaders to act without hesitation or doubt because they are not dealing with unknowns. The future, for them, is known and inevitable. They act with the knowledge that the future is already realized and that their present actions are simply part of bringing it into being.

Combined with aforethinking, aforebeing becomes the foundation for a strategic discipline that can be applied to leadership, governance, and innovation.

This discipline reframes *how* we think at long-term strategy.

Traditionally, planning involves some degree of speculation, some aleas, where outcomes are uncertain, and decisions are made based on probabilities and risk management – and often, with fear.

By accepting the future as today, leaders free themselves from the fear of failure or unforeseen complications. The process becomes one of revealing the future, rather than creating it, much like Michelangelo freeing the statue from the marble. The fear of the process fades because the outcome is no longer in doubt.

Leaders in this way welcome difficulties as a necessary part of their step forward.

From Aforethinking to Aforebeing

The transition from aforethinking to aforebeing is a natural progression in the mindset of a strategic leader. Aforethinking involves using data-driven analysis to explore multiple potential futures and identify the most probable scenario. It is the disciplined process of probability digging, where the leader builds a comprehensive understanding of possible outcomes based on available data and trends.

Once the most probable future has been identified, the leader must transition into aforebeing, where they mentally and emotionally inhabit that future. This is more than simple intuition or idealistic visioning. A real-life leader does not live in a delusional world detached from reality; instead, they make the leap from probable outcomes to embracing the inevitable future.

The Art of combining Data and Vision

In aforebeing, the leader aligns their actions and decisions with the future scenario they have chosen based on their aforethinking process.

This is where the strength of a great leader lies: in the ability to combine rigorous data analysis (aforethinking) with the clarity and conviction of aforebeing, turning vision into reality.

Leaders who embody this mindset use both rational foresight and intuitive certainty, grounding their future actions in facts while moving confidently toward a future they already see as inevitable.

Thus, aforebeing isn't just living in a future vision—it's about fully embracing that future with certainty and acting in the present to realize it, driven by both data and vision.

This synthesis of data-driven analysis and vision allows leaders to move beyond speculation and to confidently shape the present in alignment with the future they know will unfold.

So, let's now connect the dots we have traced into

A viable path

Aforethinking: Strategic Foresight and Planning

Definition:

Aforethinking is the act of anticipating the future with clarity, planning based on long-term vision, and aligning today's actions with that envisioned future. The strategist practicing aforethinking looks ahead and prepares for multiple scenarios but does so from a place of intellectual and strategic foresight.

Key Focus:

- Crafting multiple future scenarios and weighing potential outcomes.
- Building resilience and adaptability into plans.
- Using data, trends, and historical context to inform future-focused decisions.

A company planning to enter a new market may use aforethinking by analysing future market trends, customer behaviour, and potential disruptions. Based on these insights, the company strategically positions itself for long-term growth and success, rather than focusing solely on immediate returns.

Steps in Aforethinking:

1. Foresight and Analysis: The strategist gathers data and considers future trends, disruptions, and possibilities.

2. Scenario Planning: They create different models of potential futures, preparing for each one by crafting strategies for various contingencies.

3. Present Action: Current decisions are made based on how they align with the envisioned future, ensuring adaptability and resilience in execution.

Aforebeing: Living in the Future

Definition:

Aforebeing goes beyond foresight and planning—it is the state of inhabiting the future. The strategist does not simply consider what might happen; they live as though the future they envision is already a reality. From this mental position, they control the present with certainty, guiding actions as though they are inevitable steps toward that future.

Key Focus:

- Living with complete certainty in the future reality.
- Acting with purpose and clarity, as though the future has already unfolded.
- Making present-day decisions that align seamlessly with the future vision, without hesitation or doubt.

Steps in Aforebeing:

1. Future Immersion: The leader mentally and emotionally aligns with the future, behaving as though they are already living within it.

2. Present Control: this allows to shape the present with precision, knowing that today's decisions are inevitable extensions of the future.

3. Certainty in Action: The strategist operates without hesitation, as they are already certain of the outcome, guiding present efforts with confidence and strategic mastery.

Now, transitioning from aforethinking to aforebeing involves moving from intellectual foresight to existential alignment with the future, with a quantic leap.

Here's how this path unfolds:

Step 1: Strategic Foresight (Aforethinking)
- Analytical Foresight: Begin with deep analysis and foresight, using data, trends, and historical context to create a vision of the future. The strategist engages in scenario planning and risk assessment, positioning themselves to act with knowledge of potential future developments.
- Create Multiple Futures: Rather than focusing on one possible outcome, develop multiple plausible future scenarios and align strategic actions with these possibilities.

Action: For a political strategist, this means analysing future geopolitical shifts and aligning today's policies with long-term global dynamics, such as emerging powers or shifting alliances. Strategic foresight guides decisions in a way that makes the future more predictable and manageable.

Step 2: Visionary Alignment

- Select and Commit to a Future: Transitioning from aforethinking to aforebeing requires committing *to one particular future* as the inevitable reality. This is where the strategist goes beyond considering multiple options and fully immerses themselves in the certainty of a chosen future.
- Deeply Internalize the Future: The strategist now begins to act not from the mindset of "what if," but as if the future vision they have selected is already happening. This step moves beyond mere analysis—it requires emotional, intellectual, and strategic commitment to the future outcome.

Action: A business leader might see a future where artificial intelligence (AI) is integral to every industry. By internalizing this reality, they begin aligning every aspect of their company with this AI-driven future—from product development to workforce training—acting as if AI is already fully integrated into society.

Step 3: Behavioural Alignment (Bridging the Gap)
- Shape the Present through the Future: As the strategist begins to live mentally in the future, they consciously start to control the present by making decisions that feel inevitable in light of their future alignment. This is where aforebeing begins to take hold. Every decision, every move, is not speculative but is made as if the future is already certain.
- Seamless Present-Future Alignment: Actions in the present are no longer merely reactive or predictive; they are purposefully proactive, aligning with the future the strategist inhabits. There is no disconnect between where the strategist is mentally and where the world is today—because in their mind, the future has already happened.

Action: A political leader envisions a future where their nation is a global technological powerhouse. They begin investing heavily in infrastructure, education, and digital policies, not as preparatory steps but as inevitable foundations of the future state they already mentally reside in. They act with complete certainty that their vision is unfolding, controlling the present with clarity and foresight.

Step 4: Total Future Immersion (Aforebeing)
- Living One Step Forward: In this final stage, aforebeing is fully realized. The strategist is no longer merely anticipating or preparing for the future—they exist mentally and emotionally within it. From this place, they can confidently control the present because they are living as though the future has already come to pass.
- Certainty of Action: The leader acts with unwavering certainty, making present-day decisions as if they are simply unfolding the future. This level of aforebeing means that they are not influenced by short-term fluctuations or immediate concerns—they are deeply rooted in their long-term vision, guiding the present with strategic precision.

Action: A CEO, mentally inhabiting a future where climate change has reshaped the global economy, has already integrated sustainability into every aspect of their company's operations. They are not responding to current environmental regulations—they are controlling the present based on a future they believe is inevitable. Every decision is made with complete alignment to that reality.

The Benefits of Aforebeing for Strategic Leadership and Planning are multiple.

1. Clarity in Decision-Making: By mentally living in the future, strategists gain clarity in their present actions. There is no second-guessing or reactive decision-making because they are acting from a position of certainty.
2. Greater Control over the Present: Aforebeing allows leaders to shape the present with precision, aligning it seamlessly with the

future vision. This gives them greater control over outcomes and reduces the impact of short-term distractions or disruptions.

3. Increased Resilience and Confidence: Leaders practicing aforebeing operate with a sense of resilience, as they are mentally living in the future. This confidence helps them weather challenges and stay focused on their long-term objectives.

4. Strategic Mastery: Leaders who practice aforebeing have the ability to master time—they blend future vision with present action, creating a strategic advantage over those who are only reacting to current trends.

The journey from aforethinking to aforebeing is basically the path that transforms strategic planning from mere foresight to mental immersion in the future.

Aforethinking enables a leader to anticipate future possibilities, but aforebeing allows them to act as if that future is already here.

By following this path, leaders gain mastery over the present, ensuring that today's decisions align perfectly with the future they envision. It is a path of certainty, purpose, and strategic control, where the future becomes a lived reality in the mind of the strategist, guiding every present action with clarity and conviction.

Aforethinking is Rooted in Probability

- Nature: Aforethinking involves strategic foresight and the use of data, trends, and scenario planning to anticipate multiple possible futures. It's grounded in probability and preparedness—considering various scenarios and aligning actions to increase the likelihood of favourable outcomes

- Key Focus:
  o Forecasting based on trends and analysis.
  o Evaluating multiple potential futures.
  o Taking calculated risks based on what could happen.
  o Decisions are made to cover a range of possibilities, often to increase resilience and adaptability.

Example: A business might plan for future market conditions by assessing different economic scenarios. They use aforethinking to make decisions that are robust across several probable futures but remain adaptable as uncertainties unfold.

Aforebeing is Based on Clear Vision

- Nature: Aforebeing, in contrast, is rooted in a singular, clear vision of the future. The strategist is not navigating probabilities or multiple outcomes but has a strong sense of certainty about one specific future. From this position, they act as if the future is already realized, making decisions with confidence and clarity that the vision will manifest.

- Key Focus:
  o Visionary leadership where the future is seen as a certainty.
  o Present actions are not based on risk mitigation but are aligned with an inevitable future.
  o Focus on certainty and commitment, where the strategist mentally inhabits that future, controlling the present as a seamless part of that journey.

Example: An entrepreneur like Elon Musk pushes forward with space exploration or renewable energy projects, not based on multiple scenarios, but because he sees a clear future where space travel is a routine part of human life. Every decision today is made with that certainty in mind, even if it defies current market trends or probabilities.

The shift: Aforethinking vs. Aforebeing

- Decision Framework:
  - Aforethinking: Decisions are made by calculating probable outcomes and preparing for multiple futures. It is analytical, using probabilities to inform strategies.

  - Aforebeing: Decisions are based on an already-envisioned future, where the leader operates with certainty rather than navigating possibilities. It is visionary, anchored in clarity rather than calculation.

- Mindset:
  - Aforethinking: Engages with uncertainty, seeking to cover different possible outcomes and build flexible strategies that can adapt as new information emerges.

  - Aforebeing: Does not engage with uncertainty but operates from a fixed point in the future. The leader believes so fully in this vision that they act as though it is already reality, making present actions inevitable steps toward that future.

- Focus on Time:
  - Aforethinking: The leader is aware of the fluidity of time, preparing for changes and adjusting to circumstances as they unfold.

  - Aforebeing: The leader exists mentally ahead of time. They are not reacting to the present; they are shaping it based on the certainty of the future they are already living in.

In Practice

Aforethinking in Action:

- Military Strategy: In warfare, generals use aforethinking to consider possible enemy movements and outcomes. They strategize around probabilities, preparing multiple contingency plans based on what the enemy might do.

- Business Strategy: A company uses aforethinking to forecast market changes and adjust its product line, developing strategies that cover different potential economic conditions.

Aforebeing in Action:

- Visionary Leadership: A leader like Steve Jobs with the iPhone acted with aforebeing. He wasn't concerned with current market trends or competitor offerings; he had a clear vision of a future where mobile computing was seamless and ubiquitous. He acted today as if that future was certain, shaping the market around that vision.

- Social Movements: Mahatma Gandhi demonstrated aforebeing by living mentally in a future where India was free through nonviolence. He acted with the certainty of someone already inhabiting that future state, guiding the present as a realization of that vision.

Shifting from Aforethinking to Aforebeing

- Aforethinking serves as the foundation for strategic planning. It involves careful assessment, scenario-building, and preparation for various futures, ensuring resilience and adaptability.

- Aforebeing evolves from aforethinking but transcends it by committing fully to one clear vision. When a leader moves beyond calculating probabilities to acting with the certainty of a specific future, they begin to shape the present with the clarity of aforebeing.

The shift from aforethinking (probability-driven) to aforebeing (vision-driven) represents a profound change in leadership and strategy.

Both have their place in planning and decision-making, but aforebeing offers the next level of certainty, where the strategist not only anticipates the future but actively inhabits it. In this way, aforethinking ensures preparedness and flexibility, while aforebeing empowers decisive and visionary action.

Formalizing this distinction—where aforethinking is probability-based and aforebeing is vision-based—could form a cornerstone in your discipline, helping leaders understand how to transition from strategic foresight to visionary leadership.

Aforethinking - to - Aforebeing Framework
From Strategic Foresight to Visionary Leadership: the ten steps

This framework outlines the transition from aforethinking (probability-based strategic foresight) to aforebeing (vision-based living), offering a structured process for leaders and strategists to move from preparing for multiple futures to inhabiting and shaping one inevitable future.

Phase 1: Aforethinking – Strategic Foresight and Planning

Objective: Build strategic foresight and resilience by analysing potential futures based on probabilities and data, ensuring preparedness for multiple possible outcomes.

Step 1: Horizon Scanning

- Action: Analyse current trends, data, and signals from the external environment.
- Goal: Identify key trends, uncertainties, and forces that could impact the future (e.g., technological advances, economic shifts, geopolitical changes).
- Tools:
  - Trend analysis
  - Scenario planning
  - PESTLE analysis (Political, Economic, Social, Technological, Legal, Environmental)

Step 2: Scenario Development

- Action: Develop multiple future scenarios based on combinations of trends and uncertainties.

- Goal: Create a range of plausible futures to assess potential risks, opportunities, and disruptions.

- Tools:
  - Scenario matrix (mapping different futures based on key uncertainties)
  - SWOT analysis for each scenario (Strengths, Weaknesses, Opportunities, Threats)

Step 3: Strategic Risk Management

- Action: Assess the probability of each scenario and develop flexible strategies that can adapt to these various futures.

- Goal: Prioritize actions that prepare for the most likely or impactful scenarios while maintaining adaptability.

- Tools:
  - Decision trees
  - Contingency planning
  - Risk management matrix (ranking by impact and likelihood)

Step 4: Present Action Based on Future Preparedness

- Action: Implement actions that align with the most probable scenarios, ensuring resilience and flexibility to pivot when needed.

- Goal: Build strategic resilience by making decisions that cover a range of future possibilities.

- Tools:
  - Balanced scorecard
  - KPI tracking (Key Performance Indicators to monitor alignment with future scenarios)

Phase 2: Transition to Aforebeing – Commitment to Vision

Objective: Move from considering multiple possible futures to selecting one clear vision of the future. This phase involves emotional and intellectual commitment to a specific outcome.

Step 5: Future Vision Selection

- Action: Identify and commit to one dominant future from the multiple scenarios considered in aforethinking.

- Goal: Create a vision of the future that aligns with long-term goals, values, and opportunities.

- Tools:
  - Visioning workshops (engage stakeholders in shaping a shared future vision)
  - Narrative development (crafting a compelling story of the future)

Step 6: Deep Internalization of the Vision

- Action: Align all mental, emotional, and organizational energy around the selected future.

- Goal: Shift from probabilistic thinking to certainty and clarity about the future. Begin to mentally inhabit this future as though it is already real.

- Tools:

- Future-back thinking (working backward from the future to present actions)
- Immersive visualization (using visualization techniques to experience the future as if it already exists)

Step 7: Create Strategic Alignment

- Action: Adjust current strategies, resources, and operations to align with the chosen future vision.

- Goal: Ensure that all present-day actions support the inevitable unfolding of the envisioned future.

- Tools:
- Strategy realignment workshops
- Scenario pruning (eliminating less likely scenarios to focus solely on the chosen vision)

Phase 3: Aforebeing – Living in the Future and Controlling the Present

Objective: Fully inhabit the future in your mindset, behaviour, and leadership style. Act from a place of certainty, where present decisions are viewed as inevitable steps toward the realized future.

Step 8: Total Mental Immersion in the Future

- Action: Embody the future mentally and emotionally, acting as though it is already your reality.

- Goal: Fully commit to the future, seeing the present as merely a stage in its unfolding.

- Tools:

- Future-state role-playing (engage leaders in exercises where they behave as though the future has already arrived)
- Future diaries (journaling as though living in the future, describing current actions in the context of that future)

Step 9: Control the Present Through Future Vision

- Action: Make present-day decisions with the certainty that they are inevitable parts of the future you are mentally living in.

- Goal: Direct the present with precision and purpose, ensuring every action is an extension of the inevitable future.

- Tools:
- Vision-aligned decision frameworks (ensure all decisions, no matter how small, align with the chosen future)
- Strategic foresight monitoring (regularly assess the alignment of present actions with the long-term vision)

Step 10: Leading from the Future

- Action: Lead others with confidence and certainty, guiding them toward the future you have already inhabited in your mind.

- Goal: Inspire teams and organizations to act in alignment with the future vision, shaping today's actions as if they are inevitable steps toward that future.

- Tools:
- Visionary leadership development programs
- Alignment workshops (ensuring teams understand and align with the inevitable future vision)

Key Distinctions: Aforethinking vs. Aforebeing

Aspect	Aforethinking	Aforebeing
Foundation	Probability, foresight, and scenario planning	Certainty, clear vision, and mental immersion
Number of Futures	Multiple possible futures	One inevitable, clearly defined future
Decision-Making Style	Adaptive and flexible, based on probabilities	Decisive and confident, based on certainty
Mindset	Preparing for a range of outcomes	Mentally living in a singular future
Present Actions	Covering a range of possibilities	Directly aligned with the envisioned future
Leadership Approach	Analytical and strategic	Visionary and inspiring

Application of the Framework

This framework can be applied in:

- Business Strategy: Leaders transitioning from preparing for market shifts (aforethinking) to leading industry changes by acting as if they are already in the future (aforebeing).
- Political Strategy: Policymakers moving from planning for various geopolitical outcomes to governing with a vision of the future already realized.
- Personal Leadership: Individuals can use aforethinking to prepare for personal growth scenarios, then transition to aforebeing by living as though their envisioned personal or professional future is already here.

Aforethinking to Aforebeing Methodology

Define Purpose and Context

The first step is to define the context in which the methodology will be applied. This ensures that the strategic thinking or visionary process aligns with the specific goals, environment, and constraints of the user (whether an individual or organization).

Step 1.1: Identify Strategic Context
- Goal: Clarify the environment, market conditions, organizational challenges, or personal circumstances that frame the need for foresight and future-based thinking.
- Action: Conduct a comprehensive situational analysis using tools like SWOT or PESTLE analysis.
- Deliverable: A document or briefing that summarizes the external and internal factors that need to be considered in the process of aforethinking and aforebeing.

Step 1.2: Establish the Long-Term Vision or Goal
- Goal: Define the overarching vision or long-term goal that will guide the foresight and visionary leadership process.
- Action: Create a vision statement, strategic goal, or personal ambition that will serve as the focal point for the transition from aforethinking to aforebeing.
- Deliverable: A clearly articulated long-term vision that forms the foundation of all future actions.

Aforethinking: Strategic Foresight and Scenario Building

This phase introduces aforethinking, focusing on exploring probable futures and preparing for multiple potential outcomes.

Step 2.1: Horizon Scanning and Data Collection
- Goal: Gather data and intelligence on trends, disruptions, and opportunities that could impact the future in the relevant context.
- Action: Use foresight tools (trend analysis, competitive intelligence, market research) to identify key factors influencing the future.
- Deliverable: A horizon scan report highlighting the most significant trends and uncertainties.

Step 2.2: Scenario Development and Planning
- Goal: Develop multiple, plausible future scenarios that reflect a range of possible outcomes.
- Action: Build detailed future scenarios by identifying key uncertainties (e.g., economic shifts, technological breakthroughs, or geopolitical risks).
- Deliverable: A scenario matrix outlining 3–5 distinct future possibilities with strategic implications for each.

Step 2.3: Risk Assessment and Strategic Alignment
- Goal: Assess the probability and impact of each scenario to ensure the strategy is resilient across different futures.
- Action: Use tools like scenario testing, Monte Carlo simulations, or risk matrices to evaluate which scenarios are most likely and impactful.
- Deliverable: A risk assessment report, including strategic options for each scenario.

Step 2.4: Actionable Strategy
- Goal: Create a strategic plan that prepares for multiple possible futures while allowing adaptability.
- Action: Build a flexible strategy with core actions that are robust across different scenarios but adaptive to change.

- Deliverable: A strategic roadmap that outlines key initiatives, milestones, and contingency plans for different future scenarios.

Transition from Aforethinking to Aforebeing

In this phase, the methodology transitions from strategic foresight (aforethinking) to aforebeing, where the user commits to a clear vision of the future and begins to act from a place of certainty.

Step 3.1: Select and Commit to a Singular Future Vision
- Goal: Move from managing multiple futures to selecting one clear vision as the inevitable future.
- Action: Based on the scenario analysis, choose the future vision that aligns most strongly with long-term goals and potential for growth.
- Deliverable: A formal vision statement or strategic direction that articulates the future as a certainty rather than one possibility among many.

Step 3.2: Align the Organization or Individual Mindset
- Goal: Shift from a probabilistic, flexible mindset to a focused, future-living approach where decisions are based on certainty.
- Action: Conduct workshops, vision alignment exercises, or leadership briefings to ensure that all stakeholders or team members are fully committed to the future vision.
- Deliverable: A vision-alignment strategy or cultural shift plan that ensures everyone in the organization (or the individual themselves) operates with the chosen future as their mental framework.

Aforebeing: Living and Leading from the Future

In this phase, the methodology guides users into the aforebeing state, where they mentally and existentially inhabit the future they are committed to. The focus is on controlling present actions with the certainty of an already realized future.

Step 4.1: Future Immersion and Visualization
- Goal: Foster deep internalization of the future vision so that it becomes a lived reality in the minds of the leaders or individuals involved.
- Action: Engage in immersive exercises like future diaries, role-playing, or visualization techniques where participants act as though they are already living in the chosen future.
- Deliverable: A series of future-oriented workshops or exercises that build deep commitment to the vision.

Step 4.2: Vision-Driven Strategic Execution
- Goal: Execute strategies that are directly aligned with the chosen future, making decisions from a place of certainty rather than possibility.
- Action: Implement strategies, policies, and decisions based on the future vision, ensuring that actions today are inevitable extensions of the envisioned future.
- Deliverable: A strategic execution plan that directly links present initiatives to the future vision.

Step 4.3: Continuous Alignment and Monitoring
- Goal: Continuously ensure that actions and behaviours remain aligned with the future vision as time progresses.
- Action: Regularly review decisions, strategies, and operations to ensure they continue to fit with the chosen future. Adjust as necessary to maintain alignment without compromising the vision.
- Deliverable: A monitoring framework that tracks key performance indicators (KPIs) and strategic alignment with the long-term vision.

Leadership and Communication from Aforebeing

The final phase focuses on leading others and communicating with clarity and vision from the position of aforebeing. This involves not only personal leadership but also inspiring others to inhabit the same future vision.

Step 5.1: Visionary Leadership Development
- Goal: Develop leadership skills that enable clear, future-based communication and inspire others to align with the vision.
- Action: Provide leadership training, focusing on visionary thinking, communication, and strategic clarity. Leaders should be trained to guide others based on the certainty of the future they have internalized.
- Deliverable: Leadership development programs that focus on visionary thinking and future-driven leadership.

Step 5.2: Inspiring Others to Inhabit the Future
- Goal: Communicate the vision effectively to teams, stakeholders, or the public, inspiring them to act with the same certainty and alignment.
- Action: Use storytelling, vision-based communication, and motivational leadership to bring others along in the journey toward the inevitable future.
- Deliverable: A communication plan or vision statement that engages and aligns all key players with the chosen future.

Key Outcomes of the Methodology

- Resilience and Flexibility (Aforethinking): Users will be prepared for multiple potential futures, ensuring that they can adapt to changes while still moving toward long-term goals.
- Clear Vision and Certainty (Aforebeing): Users will transition to a state where they operate from a place of complete clarity and certainty about the future, guiding present actions with precision and purpose.

- Aligned Leadership and Action: Leaders and individuals will not only envision the future but inhabit it, controlling present actions as part of the inevitable unfolding of their chosen vision.

Leading from the Future

In aforebeing, the future is not a distant, speculative concept but a present reality for the strategist. It is not merely a mindset but a point of view, one in which the future is already known and inhabited.

The key question that guides every decision is not, "What will we do tomorrow?" but instead, "What did we do yesterday to arrive at this future today?"

This point of view shapes how we plan and act. The future, from this perspective, has already happened. The task is to reverse-engineer the journey back to the present, asking how each step led to the inevitable outcome we have already envisioned. In this sense, today's actions are not attempts to shape an uncertain tomorrow, but deliberate steps that align with a future already living in the planner's reality.

However, the path to that future must remain flexible. While the final destination is fixed, the steps to get there may need to adapt to unforeseen circumstances. The practical tools outlined in this chapter—Reverse Gantt, Reverse Training, and Reverse Finance—are designed to help leaders map their steps backward from the future to the present, ensuring that every action is rooted in the certainty of the outcome but adaptable in the journey.

These tools provide structure for translating the aforebeing point of view into concrete, actionable plans.

By continually asking, "What did we do yesterday to reach today?" we can maintain clarity, focus, and consistency in navigating our organizations toward the inevitable future we already inhabit.

But a strategist needs tools. Let's find out together what we have and what we shall invent.

Steps from Aforethinking to Aforebeing

The transition from aforethinking (probability-based strategic foresight) to aforebeing (vision-based certainty) involves a shift from exploring multiple potential futures to inhabiting a chosen future. These stages require different tools to navigate the complexities of the present while aligning with the future vision.

Key Steps:
1. Define Purpose and Context: Analyse the strategic environment to understand the factors shaping possible futures.
2. Aforethinking: Use data and foresight tools to build multiple potential future scenarios, assessing risks and opportunities.
3. Commit to a Singular Future: Transition from exploring options to selecting one clear, inevitable future and aligning all actions with this vision.
4. Aforebeing: Lead and act as though the future is already realized, controlling the present with certainty and purpose.
5. Monitor and Align: Continuously check that actions in the present stay aligned with the chosen future and make adjustments where necessary.

Practical Tools for Each Phase

Each phase requires specific tools tailored to either aforethinking or aforebeing. Here's a breakdown of which tools to use in each stage and how they differ:

Phase 1: Define Purpose and Context (Tools for Both Aforethinking and Aforebeing)

- SWOT Analysis (Aforethinking): In this initial phase, the classic SWOT is used to assess current strengths, weaknesses,

opportunities, and threats. This analysis helps build a picture of the present situation and what may influence future possibilities.
- PESTLE Analysis: An external analysis of the Political, Economic, Social, Technological, Legal, and Environmental factors that influence the strategic context. This tool is critical in identifying broader forces that could shape future scenarios.

Tools:
- SWOT Analysis
- PESTLE Analysis

Phase 2: Aforethinking – Strategic Foresight and Scenario Building

In this phase, the strategist explores multiple potential futures by analysing trends, identifying uncertainties, and developing a range of scenarios. The tools used here are designed to evaluate probabilities and risks, preparing for a variety of possible outcomes.

- Scenario Planning: Develop multiple future scenarios based on uncertainties. This tool helps prepare for different possibilities by exploring alternative outcomes.
- Trend Analysis: This tool analyzes market trends, technological advancements, and other data points to anticipate future changes and help create probable scenarios.
- Risk Matrices (Monte Carlo simulations, risk modeling): Used to assess the probability of each scenario and the potential impact of uncertainties. These tools ensure the strategy is resilient across various future possibilities.

Tools for Aforethinking:
- Scenario Planning
- Trend Analysis
- Risk Assessment Models (e.g., Monte Carlo)

Transition – Committing to a Singular Future

Here, the strategist transitions from evaluating multiple scenarios to selecting one inevitable future. This phase requires a different mindset and set of tools, as it marks the shift from probability to certainty.

- Vision Statement Workshops: These are collaborative sessions where a clear, singular vision of the future is articulated and committed to by all stakeholders.
- Reverse SWOT Analysis (Aforebeing): Unlike the traditional SWOT, the Reverse SWOT focuses on the certainty of the future. Opportunities reflect success in the chosen future, while threats are risks tied to potential alternative futures that need to be avoided. This ensures actions are guided away from divergent paths.

Tools for Transition:
- Vision Statement Workshops
- Reverse SWOT

Aforebeing – Living and Leading from the Future

In aforebeing, the leader operates with certainty about the future, controlling the present from the vantage point of that inevitable future. The tools here focus on reverse engineering the path from the chosen future back to today.

- Reverse Gantt: This tool maps the journey from the fixed future milestone back to the present, ensuring that today's actions align with the inevitable outcome. The flexibility lies in how to achieve milestones, but the destination remains constant.

- Reverse Finance: Instead of focusing on current financial challenges, Reverse Finance works backward from the financial success in the future. It identifies future financial goals and

tracks backward to understand the investments and decisions that led to that outcome.
- Reverse Training: This tool begins with the competencies and skills that people in the future will need. It works back to the present, identifying training needs today that will prepare individuals to succeed in the future.

Monitor and Align – Continuous Adjustment

The final phase requires ongoing monitoring to ensure that actions remain aligned with the chosen future. Even though the future is certain, the path may need adjustments due to evolving conditions. The tools here ensure continuous alignment with the strategic vision.

- KPI Dashboards: These dashboards track key performance indicators (KPIs) that measure alignment with the future vision. They allow real-time adjustments to ensure that all actions contribute to the future goal.
- Visionary Leadership Programs: These programs develop leaders who can communicate the future vision clearly and inspire others to align with it. Storytelling and future-driven communication become essential tools in keeping teams committed to the future.

Tools for Monitoring and Alignment:
- KPI Dashboards
- Visionary Leadership Development

Differentiating Tools for Aforethinking and Aforebeing

The distinction between tools used in aforethinking and aforebeing is rooted in their different focuses: aforethinking is about exploring probabilities, while aforebeing is about leading from a position of certainty.

Aforethinking Tools (Probabilities and Flexibility):
- Traditional SWOT Analysis: Focuses on identifying current opportunities and threats based on the present environment.
- Scenario Planning: Develops multiple future possibilities to prepare for various outcomes.
- Risk Assessment: Evaluates probabilities and contingencies across different futures.

Aforebeing Tools (Certainty and Control):
- Reverse SWOT: Opportunities and threats are seen from the vantage point of the chosen future, not the present. Threats represent risks that could derail the path toward that future.
- Reverse Gantt: Works backward from the future goal to ensure that present actions align with an already determined outcome.
- Reverse Training: Identifies the skills needed in the future and trains individuals accordingly today, ensuring that they are ready to inhabit the future as it unfolds.

Let's choose some of these tools for a better comprehension.

Tools for Aforebeings

Reverse SWOT: Addressing Threats to Secure the Chosen Future

In Reverse SWOT, while the strategist operates from the certainty of a pre-determined future, it is still essential to identify potential threats—not as current dangers, but as risks that could lead to alternative futures. These threats remain relevant because they represent paths that, if not avoided, could divert the strategist from their envisioned reality. Recognizing these threats ensures that actions today are taken to mitigate risks and stay aligned with the chosen future.

Threats in Reverse SWOT:

- Potential Future Divergences: In reverse SWOT, threats are seen as potential factors that could still steer the organization or individual toward an undesirable alternative future. These threats must be carefully mapped out and acknowledged, not as present-day dangers, but as risks to be actively avoided to stay aligned with the future already envisioned.

- Navigating Uncertainty: While aforebeing offers clarity about the future, threats are scenarios or obstacles that could arise if present actions deviate from the chosen path. Identifying them allows the strategist to steer clear of decisions or actions that could open the door to unwanted outcomes.

- Proactive Mitigation: The threats in Reverse SWOT are future obstacles that have been recognized from a vantage point of certainty. Instead of reacting to these threats, the strategist proactively takes steps to eliminate or neutralize them early, ensuring they do not disrupt the progression toward the chosen future.

Practical Example of Reverse SWOT Threats: In a company envisioning itself as a leader in AI by 2030, threats could include:

- Regulatory changes that could slow down innovation or restrict the company's operations.

- Technological breakthroughs by competitors that challenge the company's market position.

While these threats are potential risks, identifying them ensures that the strategist can develop plans to prevent them from materializing, securing the company's path to the future it envisions. In this way, threats serve as guardrails, reminding the strategist what to avoid while staying committed to the future they inhabit.

By incorporating threats as divergent possibilities in the Reverse SWOT, the strategist can ensure that they remain vigilant in their actions, proactively shaping the present to prevent alternative futures from arising.

Gantt and Reverse Gantt: A Powerful Tool of Check and Balance

The simultaneous use of Gantt charts (from aforethinking) and Reverse Gantt charts (from aforebeing) is a powerful mechanism for maintaining strategic alignment between the probability-based foresight and the certainty-driven future vision. Their intersection in time creates an opportunity for continuous check and balance, ensuring that planning (aforethinking) and control (aforebeing) work in harmony.

Alignment as a Strategic Imperative

When the timelines and milestones of a Gantt and Reverse Gantt are in sync, they signal that the present actions, planned for multiple possible futures, are fully aligned with the future outcome the strategist has already embraced. However, if misalignment occurs—if the milestones do not overlap or actions diverge—this reveals that there is a gap between foresight and certainty, or between probability and vision.

Diagnosing and Correcting Misalignment

If the Gantt and Reverse Gantt become misaligned, it is a crucial signal that the current strategies, decisions, or actions are not effectively guiding the organization toward the envisioned future. In this case, the gap must be studied carefully, asking key questions:

1. Where is the Misalignment? Identify which actions or milestones in the Gantt chart (probability-based planning) do not align with the reverse Gantt's fixed future milestones.

2. Why Does the Misalignment Exist? Is the misalignment due to unexpected external factors, a flaw in the original foresight, or an internal factor such as resource allocation or execution challenges?

3. Corrective Actions: Once the misalignment is identified, corrective actions should be taken to recalibrate the foresight tools (Gantt) and adapt the present decisions to realign with the future vision. This process ensures that today's actions remain relevant, flexible, and effectively guided toward the inevitable future the strategist inhabits.

Strategy example

Consider a company transitioning toward renewable energy by 2030:

- The Gantt chart (aforethinking) projects various potential steps for entering new markets and launching products, allowing flexibility based on evolving market conditions.
- The Reverse Gantt chart (aforebeing) begins at the 2030 goal—domination in the renewable energy market—and works backward to ensure that every action aligns with this future.

Misalignment between the two could indicate that current steps are deviating from the fixed future outcome, such as delays in product development or regulatory hurdles. By analysing this misalignment, the company can adjust its actions to ensure milestones are met, staying on course for the future it has already envisioned.

Gantt and Reverse Gantt as Continuous Checks

The alignment between Gantt and Reverse Gantt serves as an ongoing check and balance system, helping leaders ensure that strategic foresight and vision-driven certainty remain in sync. When used together, these tools foster a robust framework for dynamic planning, allowing the flexibility to adapt to present conditions while remaining focused on the inevitable future. Misalignments are not failures but opportunities for course correction, ensuring that decisions today are always leading toward tomorrow's success.

The Reverse Gantt: A Future-Led Approach to Strategic Planning

The Reverse Gantt is a project management tool designed to work backward from a future goal to the present, ensuring that each step aligns with the eventual outcome. Unlike a traditional Gantt chart that plots a timeline from today toward a future goal, the Reverse Gantt starts with the final milestone—the future vision or outcome—and traces each prior step back to the current day.

This approach is particularly valuable in the context of aforebeing, where the future is not seen as speculative but as certain and pre-determined. The Reverse Gantt enables leaders and strategists to align their current actions with that inevitable future, providing clarity on what must be done today to realize that future.

Key Components of the Reverse Gantt

1. Future Milestone as the Starting Point
   - The Reverse Gantt begins with a clearly defined future goal or outcome, which could be a business objective, strategic initiative, or personal target. This future is not aspirational—it is the inevitable reality the strategist has chosen to inhabit. For example, a company might envision being the market leader in a specific industry by 2030.

2. Mapping the Steps in Reverse
   - Once the future goal is established, the strategist maps backward the necessary steps, initiatives, or milestones that led to that success. For each milestone, the question becomes: What did we need to accomplish just before this? This process ensures that every action taken today is an essential part of the larger strategic plan.

3. Identifying Dependencies
- Dependencies between tasks are carefully mapped out, ensuring that each action has the resources, time, and support it needs. For instance, if a company needs a new product line to reach its future goals, the Reverse Gantt helps trace backward the research, development, and market entry strategies that led to that product launch.

4. Current Actions Driven by Future Certainty
- Unlike traditional project management, which adapts the future to fit present realities, the Reverse Gantt demands that today's actions conform to the certainty of the future. This allows for greater alignment, where decisions are not speculative but purposeful, based on the inevitable unfolding of the future goal.

Practical Example: A Renewable Energy Company's Reverse Gantt

Imagine a renewable energy company with a goal of becoming the market leader in solar technology by 2030. The Reverse Gantt would begin with this 2030 milestone and work backward to today, defining each step along the way:

1. 2030 – Market Leader in Solar Technology
- Strategic Milestone: By 2030, the company has solidified its position as the market leader in solar energy technology. It boasts innovative solar panels, strong industry partnerships, and an expansive global customer base. This leadership is characterized by cutting-edge product offerings, sustainable practices, and dominance in both developed and emerging markets.

2. 2027 – Solar Energy Facility Fully Operational
- Strategic Milestone: The solar energy facility is fully operational and producing substantial energy output. By 2027, the

company has successfully transitioned from R&D and construction phases to large-scale energy production. The solar energy produced is now powering homes and businesses while earning carbon credits for the company.

3. 2026 – Final Construction Phase
   - Strategic Milestone: The company has completed the last phases of construction for the solar facility. All systems are in place, and the facility is prepared to begin full-scale production. Final touches on infrastructure, regulatory approvals, and partnerships with suppliers are solidified by this stage.

4. 2025 – Land Acquisition and Early Construction
   - Strategic Milestone: The company secures the necessary land and begins early construction of its solar facility. This stage includes breaking ground on the new project, completing initial infrastructure, and establishing essential partnerships with local suppliers and governments.

5. 2024 – Research and Development
   - Strategic Milestone: In 2024, the company's R&D efforts are centred around breakthrough solar panel technology and energy storage innovations. The R&D team is focused on solving technical challenges and finalizing the prototypes that will be developed into full-scale products by 2027. This phase is critical for ensuring that the solar panels are both technologically advanced and cost-effective for large-scale production.

With this Reverse Gantt, the company now knows that today's focus must be on assembling an expert R&D team, securing partnerships, and laying the groundwork for technological breakthroughs. The certainty of the 2030 future goal informs every action in the present.

The Reverse Gantt is not just a timeline tool—it is a strategic alignment mechanism. It ensures that present actions are not just driven by current trends or reactive decisions but are directly influenced by a clear, pre-determined future.

This process helps:
- Avoid deviation: It becomes clear when current actions are misaligned with the ultimate goal, as the reverse mapping keeps the strategy focused.

- Guide decision-making: The Reverse Gantt helps prioritize actions based on their importance to the future goal.

- Adapt while maintaining focus: Even as external conditions change, the overarching future remains fixed, ensuring that while the how may shift, the what and why stay constant.

When the Reverse Gantt and Traditional Gantt Overlap

When both the Gantt chart (aforethinking) and the Reverse Gantt (aforebeing) overlap in the same time span, they offer a powerful check and balance. If both tools are aligned, the actions planned today are clearly leading toward the chosen future. However, if they are misaligned, it signals a potential flaw in the foresight or a disconnect between the future vision and current execution.

In such cases, leaders must examine the misalignment to identify:

- Why the gap exists: Is it due to an external shift, misjudgement in foresight, or an execution failure?

- How to correct the course: Adjust the present actions or revisit the foresight to bring the Gantt and Reverse Gantt into alignment.

This balance ensures that the strategist operates with both flexibility and certainty, allowing for adjustments while staying focused on the fixed future goal.

A Roadmap from the Future

The Reverse Gantt is a tool of profound strategic clarity, guiding today's actions by looking at them from the certainty of tomorrow. By starting with the future and working backward, leaders ensure that their present efforts are not speculative but firmly grounded in the vision of a future that is already determined in their mind. This approach allows for practical flexibility while maintaining an unwavering focus on the ultimate goal, transforming strategy into an active, forward-driven process.

Reverse Finance: Aligning Financial Instruments with Strategic Planning

In the context of reverse planning, finance is perhaps the most critical element because it provides the structural backbone to the strategic timeline. Unlike other resources, financial resources can be precisely mapped and planned with foresight, using a range of financial instruments and structures that allow for predictable cash flows, capital investments, and risk management over time.

The essence of Reverse Finance lies in ensuring that cash flows and financial resources are available at every point of the Reverse Gantt timeline, supporting each key milestone backward from the future goal to the present. This consistency of financial planning allows the strategist to choose the right financial instruments that align with each phase of the strategy, ensuring liquidity and financial strength at every stage of implementation.

Why Financial Planning is Essential in Reverse Strategy

Finance is unique in that it is the only element of a business strategy that can be precisely structured and aligned with future milestones. With the appropriate mix of equity, debt, and financial instruments, the strategist can ensure that capital is available at the right time and under the right terms to support each step toward the chosen future.

If finance becomes misaligned—whether through a cash flow shortage or inappropriate capital structure—the entire strategic plan risks falling apart, regardless of how well other elements like operations or marketing are managed. Hence, finance acts as the bedrock of certainty, ensuring the future vision is achievable through carefully managed resources.

Financial Instruments in Reverse Finance

In reverse planning, specific financial instruments and structures need to be chosen based on the future financial needs of the organization, not just its present situation. The following are critical financial tools that support reverse financial planning:

1. *Debt Financing*

- Corporate Bonds: These long-term debt instruments allow a company to secure funds today while paying interest over time, aligning well with a future-focused strategy. Bonds are an excellent choice when the company expects to achieve significant cash flows in the future that will cover the interest and principal repayment.

- Term Loans: Fixed-term loans allow for a predictable repayment schedule. These can be useful when a company needs to invest heavily today (e.g., in R&D or infrastructure) but expects returns from the investment in the future. The Reverse Gantt will map when cash flows are expected, allowing the company to time its loan repayment structure accordingly.

- Syndicated Loans: For large-scale projects requiring significant capital, syndicated loans involve a group of lenders sharing the risk. These are useful when the company's reverse financial planning requires large, upfront investments, such as infrastructure development, which will generate returns over time.

2. *Equity Financing*

- Venture Capital and Private Equity: If the company's future strategy requires aggressive growth or new markets, equity financing through venture capital or private equity can inject cash without adding debt to the balance sheet. This is particularly valuable in phases of the Reverse Gantt where the company needs to fund expansion or innovation without committing to debt repayments.

- Public Equity (IPO): If the reverse strategy includes a future initial public offering (IPO), equity funding can be strategically planned. By aligning public listing dates with future milestones (e.g., product launches or market expansions), the company can use the public market to raise significant capital to sustain its long-term vision.

3. Hybrid Financing Instruments

- Convertible Bonds: These instruments allow for debt to be converted into equity, which is useful in situations where the company expects significant value appreciation in the future. Convertible bonds offer flexibility—they provide debt capital now with the potential to convert into equity later, depending on future outcomes.

- Mezzanine Financing: A hybrid between debt and equity, mezzanine financing is particularly valuable for companies needing flexible capital with minimal immediate cash outflow. It is often used for growth stages, where returns are expected in the longer term, aligning perfectly with a reverse financial strategy.

- Asset-Backed Securities (ABS): These are financial securities backed by future cash flows from specific assets, such as loans or receivables. ABS allows a company to raise capital by securitizing income-generating assets. In a reverse finance strategy, ABS ensures liquidity for projects mapped in the Reverse Gantt, allowing funds to be raised for long-term investments while providing a steady income stream over time.

- Asset-Backed Funds (ABF): ABF pools together asset-backed securities to provide diversified and structured liquidity. This tool helps fund multiple projects within an organization, offering flexibility and ensuring that critical milestones on the Reverse Gantt timeline are financially supported. ABFs allow for the bundling of risks across various assets, making them valuable for ensuring cash flow consistency in complex projects.

4. Risk Management Instruments

- edging and Derivatives: Hedging strategies are critical in managing interest rate risk, currency risk, or commodity risk. By using futures contracts, options, or swaps, companies can protect their future cash flows against fluctuations that could threaten the reverse plan's financial stability.

- Insurance Solutions: Custom insurance policies, such as political risk insurance or business interruption insurance, allow companies to protect their future financial interests, ensuring they can deliver on the reverse Gantt milestones even if unforeseen risks occur.

- Real-D: A decentralized investment protection smart contract system designed to mitigate investment risk by offering a fallback mechanism. Real-D creates a safeguard against sudden devaluation in volatile assets such as cryptocurrencies, NFTs, or other digital assets. It allows investors to stack a portion of their assets as collateral, which can activate during downturns, providing stability and recovery time for strategic actions

5. Innovative Financial Instruments

In addition to traditional and hybrid instruments, innovative financial instruments offer even greater flexibility, especially when dealing with sustainable development goals, future-driven business models, or digital assets. PerValue and CleCoin provide future-focused financing options that align perfectly with the Reverse Finance strategy, offering customized tools that adapt to the future realities and milestones planned through the Reverse Gantt.

- PerValue: An innovative financial instrument, PerValue ties investment returns to specific value-based outcomes, such as social impact, sustainability, or governance achievements. This tool allows businesses to raise funds today by promising returns based on the realization of these future societal goals. PerValue integrates seamlessly with reverse finance as it enables forward-looking organizations to secure funding aligned with their long-term social impact goals, while ensuring that capital flow matches future milestones in the Reverse Gantt.

- CleCoin: A blockchain-based token, CleCoin enables companies to raise capital today based on future clean energy production or carbon credits. In the reverse finance framework, CleCoin is invaluable for projects aimed at sustainability and environmental impact, such as renewable energy plants or carbon-offset initiatives. By issuing CleCoins, organizations can raise immediate capital through a secure and transparent blockchain system, while ensuring that funding and cash flows are available when critical project milestones are reached.

Aligning Financial Instruments with the Reverse Gantt

The reverse financial approach ensures that each financial decision today supports a future milestone mapped in the Reverse Gantt. Financial instruments must be chosen based on the future point where capital is needed, not just immediate cash flow requirements.

Example of Reverse Gantt and Financial Alignment

A clean energy company has the future vision of launching a new solar energy facility by 2027 to support global expansion and contribute to sustainability goals. In reverse financial planning, the following approach can be taken:

1. **2027 – Solar Energy Facility Fully Operational**
   The company expects substantial revenue from energy production and carbon credits as the facility becomes fully operational. To finance this, PerValue could be used to align returns with value-based outcomes, such as carbon emissions reduction or clean energy generation. In 2024, corporate bonds could also be issued to raise capital for construction, with repayments structured to align with expected future revenue from energy sales and sustainability credits.

2. **2026 – Final Construction Phase**
   By this stage, the company may leverage syndicated loans to cover final construction costs, ensuring sufficient cash flow. Additionally, CleCoin can be issued immediately after the successful confirmation of R&D feasibility (in 2025), allowing the company to raise immediate capital by pre-selling carbon credits or future clean energy production. The token redemptions and cash inflows will align with the revenue streams expected after 2027.

3. **2025 – Land Acquisition and Early Construction**
   Early construction phases can be financed through venture capital or equity financing, ensuring that capital outlays during this period do not overly burden the balance sheet. Asset-backed securities (ABS) could also be employed at this stage, allowing the company to securitize future energy production or carbon credit earnings, offering investors a stake in future cash flows while freeing up early-stage capital.

4. **2024 – Research and Development**
   R&D investments during this phase will focus on advanced solar technologies and energy storage solutions. Once R&D confirms the feasibility of the project, the company can initiate the issuance of CleCoin, providing tokens that represent future

energy production and raising capital to fund the next stage of development. R&D will be financed through mezzanine financing or convertible bonds, given the high-risk, high-reward nature of these investments.

Why Consistency in Cash Flow Matters

The ultimate aim of reverse finance is to ensure that cash flows are consistent with the Reverse Gantt milestones. If financial resources are misaligned—if cash is not available when needed—it risks derailing the entire strategy. By carefully selecting the right financial instruments, the company can create a steady flow of capital, ensuring that every point in the strategy is adequately funded. Reverse Finance provides the structural integrity required to execute a reverse planning strategy. By choosing the right financial instruments and aligning cash flows with strategic milestones, leaders can ensure that every step in the Reverse Gantt is backed by the necessary resources. This financial alignment is essential to realizing the future vision, providing a framework for consistent funding, risk management, and strategic flexibility.

Financial planning, when done backward from the future to the present, ensures that today's financial decisions are in perfect alignment with tomorrow's strategic success. So, here are the aligned reverse gantts;

2030 – Market Leader in Solar Technology

- Strategic Milestone: By 2030, the company has achieved dominance in the solar energy market, offering cutting-edge solar panel technology, industry partnerships, and a strong customer base. The company's operations have fully matured, and its position as a global leader is cemented by both technological superiority and sustainable energy production.

- Financial Alignment: The company's long-term revenue generation from energy sales, sustainability credits, and carbon trading markets sustains ongoing operations. PerValue continues to align returns with value-based outcomes, such as maintaining leadership in green technology and sustainability. CleCoin is also fully integrated, used for seamless carbon credit trading and revenue generation.

2027 – Solar Energy Facility Fully Operational

- Strategic Milestone: The solar energy facility is now fully operational, producing substantial energy output and generating revenue through energy sales and carbon credits. This milestone marks the company's successful entry into full-scale production and sustainability markets.

- Financial Alignment: To finance the facility's operations, PerValue was utilized earlier (in 2024) to align returns with carbon emission reductions and clean energy generation. Additionally, corporate bonds issued in 2024 provided the capital for construction, with principal repayments aligned to the expected revenue surge starting from 2027.

2026 – Final Construction Phase

- Strategic Milestone: The company completes the final stages of construction, ensuring all systems and facilities are ready for full-scale operations. Final supplier contracts, infrastructure readiness, and regulatory compliance are critical tasks.

- Financial Alignment: During this phase, the company leverages syndicated loans to cover remaining construction costs, ensuring liquidity is maintained. CleCoin is issued after the successful confirmation of R&D feasibility in 2025, allowing the company to raise capital by pre-selling future energy production and carbon credits. Token redemptions align with revenue streams expected after 2027.

2025 – Land Acquisition and Early Construction

- Strategic Milestone: The company secures land and begins construction of the solar energy facility, establishing critical infrastructure and partnerships with local suppliers. By this time, the foundation is laid for the subsequent phases of construction and development.

- Financial Alignment: Early capital requirements are met through venture capital or equity financing, and asset-backed securities (ABS) could be employed to securitize future energy production or carbon credit earnings, offering investors a stake in future cash flows while freeing up capital for early construction stages.

2024 – Research and Development

- Strategic Milestone: The company focuses on R&D efforts aimed at advancing solar panel technology and energy storage solutions. Breakthroughs in this phase are critical for differentiating the company's solar products in the market.

- Financial Alignment: Upon confirming R&D feasibility, the company issues CleCoin to raise capital for further development. This token pre-sells future clean energy production and generates cash flow. Mezzanine financing and convertible bonds help fund this phase, providing flexible capital for high-risk, high-reward technological innovations.

Reverse Training: A Future-Oriented Framework

In reverse training, the point of view (PoW) is rooted in the future. Every decision and action are derived from a clear understanding of the future state of the organization and its workforce. By starting with a fully realized future in mind, reverse training enables leaders to shape the present to ensure that the workforce evolves in alignment with the long-term vision.

Unlike traditional training programs, which react to present needs, reverse training begins by *inhabiting* the future—examining the skills, competencies, and behaviours that define success in that future—and works backward to implement the necessary interventions today. The reverse training process is built on the certainty that the future is already determined and that the task at hand is ensuring that the present workforce can meet the demands of that future.

Phases of Reverse Training

Phase 1: Competency Observation from the Future

In reverse training, the journey begins with a thorough analysis of the future state of the workforce. We shall ask ourselves:

- *What actions are people performing in this future?*
- *What skills, both hard and soft, are required to perform these actions?*
- *What competencies define success in this afore strategic landscape?*

This phase is about observing the future as if it were the present. Leaders must mentally inhabit the future and examine the roles, behaviours, and skills of their teams to determine the competencies that drive the organization's success. The goal is to clearly identify the *future-ready* workforce and what enables them to perform at their peak.

Key Activities in Phase 1:
- Identify hard skills such as technological expertise, data literacy, or advanced problem-solving, based on the expected future challenges and opportunities.
- Assess soft skills such as adaptability, leadership, and collaboration that will allow individuals to thrive in a dynamic future environment.
- Clarify future roles and responsibilities, understanding how these competencies apply to new and evolving roles within the organization.

Phase 2: Defining the Competency Gaps

Once the necessary future competencies are clearly defined, the next step is to assess the gap between the current workforce and the future workforce.

The focus is not just on identifying the present deficiencies, but on reverse-engineering the skills and knowledge that must be built over time to meet future needs.
From the future point of view, the question is:

"What did we do over the past years to bridge the gap and ensure that our employees gained these critical skills?"

The aim of this phase is to map out the competencies that the workforce will need and create a structured development path that allows employees to evolve their skills as the organization progresses toward its future goals.

Key Activities in Phase 2:

- Evaluate current skills and compare them to the competencies required in the future. This analysis focuses on understanding the gaps that must be filled.
- Prioritize training and development areas that will enable the workforce to evolve in line with the future vision. This includes both individual skills and organizational capabilities.
- Develop a competency framework that outlines the necessary skills and behaviours, linking them to the future roles and responsibilities.

Phase 3: Action Planning for Skill Development

In this phase, the focus shifts to mapping the steps required to develop the necessary skills over time. Working backward from the future, leaders must create a detailed plan that outlines how the workforce will evolve.
The key question from the future Point of View is:

"What actions did we take to ensure our employees gained the skills they needed at each critical milestone?"

This phase emphasizes *alignment* between the Reverse Gantt and the development timeline, ensuring that the workforce evolves at the same pace as the organization's strategic objectives.

Key Activities in Phase 3:
- Design learning programs and development initiatives that align with the future competencies, ensuring that both hard and soft skills are cultivated in a structured manner over time.
- Establish a timeline for skill development that reflects the reverse timeline of the organization's strategic plan. Key milestones must align with future-ready skills.
- Monitor progress continuously, ensuring that employees are advancing in their skills development in alignment with the reverse strategy.

Phase 4: Managing Workforce Continuity and Turnover

As the future unfolds, it is inevitable that workforce turnover will occur. This phase ensures that turnover is managed in such a way that it does not disrupt the future vision. From the perspective of 2030, we look back and ask:
- *What systems did we put in place to ensure a smooth transition of talent and knowledge?*

Workforce turnover can be both a risk and an opportunity. By developing robust succession plans and training programs, the organization can ensure continuity in its leadership and technical capabilities. This phase also considers how knowledge is passed from one generation of employees to the next.

Key Activities in Phase 4:
- Plan for succession by identifying future leaders early and preparing them for key roles, ensuring leadership continuity.
- Develop mentorship programs to foster knowledge transfer from experienced employees to newer recruits, ensuring that organizational knowledge is retained.
- Manage workforce turnover by implementing a system that anticipates retirements and exits, aligning new hires with the skills and competencies needed in the future.

Phase 5: Selection and Recruitment for the Future Workforce

Finally, recruitment is key to ensuring that new talent is aligned with the future vision. From the future point of view, the question is:

"How did we select and recruit people who would be able to grow into the competencies required for the future?"

In this phase, recruitment focuses on identifying candidates who possess both the potential to develop the necessary skills and the cultural alignment with the future direction of the organization.

Key Activities in Phase 5:
- Create a recruitment strategy that prioritizes future competencies over immediate needs, ensuring that new hires are aligned with long-term goals.
- Establish selection criteria that focus on future adaptability, leadership potential, and technical expertise.
- Build a talent pipeline that ensures the continuous flow of qualified candidates capable of growing into the future workforce.

Reverse training is a future-driven approach to workforce development that ensures that the competencies required in the future are cultivated through a systematic and proactive process. Each phase of the reverse training framework—from competency observation to recruitment—is designed to ensure that the workforce is fully aligned with the long-term vision of the organization.

By beginning with a fully realized future and working backward to the present, reverse training allows leaders to anticipate and address the skill needs of tomorrow, ensuring that their teams are prepared to meet the challenges and seize the opportunities that lie ahead. This structured approach to workforce planning ensures not only that employees grow in their capabilities but also that the organization evolves with strategic precision towards its future vision.

Point of View: 2030

In 2030, the company is at the forefront of solar energy technology. Employees are innovating, managing complex systems, and collaborating across diverse, global teams. The workforce possesses a mix of technical expertise, leadership, and adaptability, with a strong focus on sustainability and innovation. To ensure that this is the reality in 2030, we need to assess the competencies, both hard and soft, that make this possible.

Step 1: Assessing Competencies in 2030

Actions Observed in 2030
- R&D Leadership: Employees are leading innovation in solar panel technology, with a deep understanding of emerging energy storage systems, photovoltaic technology, and clean energy regulations.
- Project Management: Teams are managing large-scale solar projects, coordinating complex logistics, and ensuring that every phase of energy production, from facility management to distribution, runs smoothly.
- Global Collaboration: Employees work across international borders, requiring cross-cultural communication skills, fluency in multiple languages, and digital collaboration expertise.
- Sustainability Focus: All employees understand the importance of sustainability and are committed to minimizing environmental impact through energy production and operations.
- Soft Skills: Leadership, adaptability, and emotional intelligence are paramount. The ability to lead through uncertainty, collaborate in diverse teams, and inspire innovation are essential soft skills observed in the workforce.

Step 2: Defining Hard and Soft Skills for 2030

Hard Skills
- Advanced Solar Technology: Deep knowledge in photovoltaic technology, energy storage systems, and renewable energy regulations.
- Data Analytics: Expertise in data science to monitor energy production efficiency, predict market trends, and optimize energy distribution.
- Engineering and Facility Management: Practical engineering skills, with experience in large-scale energy facility management and infrastructure development.
- Software Proficiency: Mastery of industry-specific software for energy management, facility automation, and international regulatory compliance systems.

Soft Skills
- Leadership and Emotional Intelligence: Ability to lead teams with empathy, make decisions under uncertainty, and inspire innovation.
- Cross-Cultural Communication: Fluency in multiple languages and the ability to navigate cultural differences, essential for global teamwork.
- Problem-Solving and Adaptability: Quick thinking, adaptability to changing technologies, and the ability to find solutions to complex challenges.
- Sustainability Mindset: A deep commitment to sustainability and environmental stewardship, integrating these values into daily work.

Step 3: Planning the Actions for Skills Development (2025-2029)
Now, we must plan backward to ensure that employees in 2030 have the skills and mindset required. The following actions will be put in place over time to ensure this:

2029 – Final Preparations for Full-Scale Future Workforce
- Advanced Leadership Programs: Offer leadership development initiatives focusing on future-oriented leadership, sustainability integration, and managing innovation.
- Global Team Collaboration Simulations: Run simulations for international teams to build collaboration and digital communication proficiency.
- Sustainability Workshops: Ensure all employees are well-versed in sustainability practices, integrating these into their daily operations and decision-making processes.

2027 – Intermediate Skills and Competencies
- Cross-Functional Project Teams: Introduce cross-departmental projects to foster collaboration and flexibility among teams. Encourage learning from other disciplines like data science and engineering.
- Tech Mastery Workshops: Train employees in advanced photovoltaic and energy storage technology, making sure they are proficient in current and emerging technologies.
- Soft Skills Development: Incorporate mandatory training in cross-cultural communication, problem-solving, and adaptability to ensure employees can thrive in global teams.

2025 – Early Training and Development
- Graduate Programs and Internships: Establish partnerships with leading universities to recruit top talent early, offering graduate programs focused on energy technology and sustainability.
- Online Learning Platforms: Provide accessible, ongoing online education platforms where employees can continuously learn and upgrade their skills in advanced solar technology, project management, and leadership.
- Data and Engineering Bootcamps: Offer intensive bootcamps for data analysis and engineering to upskill existing employees or prepare new hires for roles in solar energy projects.

Step 4: Addressing Turnover and Workforce Continuity (2025-2029)

2028-2029 – Succession Planning and Knowledge Transfer
- Mentorship Programs: Senior leaders mentor younger employees, ensuring that critical knowledge and skills are passed down.
- Knowledge Management Systems: Implement platforms where knowledge and innovations are documented, allowing future generations of employees to learn from past projects.
- Succession Plans: Create robust succession plans, identifying future leaders who will drive innovation and operations beyond 2030.

2025-2027 – Addressing Turnover through Skills Bridging

- Targeted Recruitment: Focus recruitment efforts on filling skill gaps identified through regular workforce assessments.
- Onboarding and Upskilling for New Recruits: Ensure new hires receive rigorous onboarding and targeted upskilling in photovoltaic technology, data analytics, and sustainability.
- Employee Retention Initiatives: Offer incentives, career progression opportunities, and work-life balance programs to reduce turnover and keep top talent engaged.

Step 5: Selection Parameters for Future HR (2024)

By 2024, the groundwork must be laid for selecting candidates who are capable of developing the competencies needed for 2030.

Selection Criteria for 2024 HR

- Tech-Savvy Innovators: Prioritize candidates with strong backgrounds in engineering, data science, or solar technology.

Look for individuals who are adaptable and excited about innovation.

- Sustainability Advocates: Select candidates who demonstrate a clear passion for sustainability and a history of implementing sustainable practices in their previous roles.

- Leadership Potential: Identify individuals with a high emotional intelligence quotient (EQ), problem-solving abilities, and leadership potential, focusing on those who can lead teams and innovate under pressure.

- Cultural Fit and Global Mindset: Ensure that candidates possess strong cross-cultural communication skills and a global perspective, capable of thriving in diverse teams across different geographies.

These examples should help us to build our own set of tools to achieve practical aforebeing.

Naturally, I am the second-best person in this world interested in knowing about these tools.

The first one is, naturally, you.

The future is

As we stand at the crossroads of decision, remember that true leadership is not about navigating the currents of today's uncertainty.

It is about inhabiting the future that we dare to believe in.

The future is not some distant place we are heading toward: it already lives within us, waiting to be revealed.

Like Michelangelo freeing the angel from the marble, the future is not hidden from us—it is already formed, already realized in the core of our being. All we must do is have the courage to reveal it.

In the silence of our thoughts, we begin by foreseeing the possibilities—aforethinking, guided by the patterns, by the data, by the maps of our past.

But soon, we realize something greater: the future we are anticipating is not a shadow we are chasing, but a light we already carry. That light, that certainty, is what allows us to transition from thinking to being. We shift from navigating the probabilities of many futures to fully embracing the one future that calls us most powerfully.

In this space, there is no hesitation. There is no fear. For in aforebeing, we are not waiting for the future to arrive. We are already there. We breathe it. We live it. The decisions we make today are not speculative—they are the inevitable steps of a journey we are already on.

To lead is to live one step forward, to act with the confidence of hindsight in a moment that others see as uncertain. Like the great artists and visionaries before us, who knew their path as though it had already unfolded, we too must carve out the present with the assurance of a future that we have already touched. And in doing so, we do not merely prepare for the future—we create it, moment by moment, with every choice we make.

So, just embrace the future that lies within you, or better let it live throughout your being. Let aforethinking guide you to the door, and let aforebeing lead you through it.

The future is not somewhere out there — it is here, now.

Marco Palombi

Bibliography

1. Vasari, G. (1991). *The Lives of the Artists*. Oxford University Press. (Original work published 1568).
2. Kennedy, J. F. (1961). *Special Message to the Congress on Urgent National Needs*. John F. Kennedy Presidential Library and Museum.
3. Churchill, W. (1946). *The Sinews of Peace ("Iron Curtain Speech")*. Westminster College, Fulton, Missouri.
4. Michelangelo. *Selected Works*. (Michelangelo's personal notes and works are frequently referenced in art history textbooks and scholarly journals).
5. Bismarck, O. von. (1862). *Blood and Iron Speech*. (Original transcript available through primary historical resources).
6. Metternich, K. (1815). *Congress of Vienna Papers*. (Available through European diplomatic history archives).
7. Medici, L. (1480). *Correspondences*. (Collected in various historical texts concerning Renaissance Florence).
8. Windsor, H.R.H. Queen Elizabeth II (2022). *The House of Windsor: Crisis and Adaptation in Modern Times*. Oxford University Press.
9. Palombi, M. (2024). *CleCoin: Blockchain and Renewable Energy Finance*.
10. Palombi, M. (2024). *PerValue Whitepaper: A New Financial Instrument for Impact-Driven Investments*.
11. Palombi, M. (2024). *Real-D: A Financial Risk Management Solution*.
12. Deutsche Bank Research (2023). *ABS and ABF: Structuring Asset-Backed Securities and Asset-Backed Funds*. DB Publications.
13. Johnson, T. (2021). *Strategic Foresight and Scenario Planning for Business Leaders*. McKinsey Quarterly.

Reader's notes

Reader's notes

www.ingramcontent.com/pod-product-compliance
Lightning Source LLC
Chambersburg PA
CBHW070356230526
45471CB00006B/2599